7

BILINGUAL SONGS

English-French vol. 4

by
Marie-France Marcie
Music by Sara Jordan

Produced and Published by
Sara Jordan Publishing
a division of ℗©2006 Jordan Music Productions Inc.
(SOCAN)

ISBN 1-55386-050-0

Acknowledgments

Lyricist - Marie-France Marcie

Editor - Véronique Ponce

Producer - Sara Jordan

Music Co-producer, Arranger, Engineer - Mark Shannon

Male Singer - Peter LeBuis

Female Singer - Julie Crochetière

Illustrations - Jessica Jordan-Brough

Cover Design and Layout - Campbell Creative Services

Digitally Recorded and Mixed by Mark Shannon,
The TreeFort, Toronto, Ontario.

For further information contact:

Jordan Music Productions Inc.
M.P.O. Box 490
Niagara Falls, NY
U.S.A. 14302-0490

Jordan Music Productions Inc.
Station M, Box 160
Toronto, Ontario
Canada, M6S 4T3

Internet: http://www.sara-jordan.com
e-mail: sjordan@sara-jordan.com
Telephone: 1-800-567-7733

To my daughters

À mes filles

Recommended Companion

We suggest purchasing our campanion resource book, *Bilingual Kids English-French, vol. 4,* which has lessons, activities and reproducible exercises reinforcing the material taught in these songs.

For more information please visit
www.SongsThatTeach.com

or call us toll free
1-800-567-7733

The translation of these bilingual songs is close in most cases, however, in some verses similar words and arrangement of the words were used to obtain better musical results.

We acknowledge the financial support of the Government of Canada through the Book Publishing Industry Development Program (BPIDP) for our publishing activities.

Contents/ *Table des matières*

Hints for Teachers and Parents

Bilingual Songs: English- French, vol. 4, has been developed for use by second language learners as well as instructors, parents and teachers.

These songs, featuring curriculum based content, offer an attractive and easy-to-use format that facilitates learning in both French and English.

Complying with the five major principles of the Standards of Foreign Language Learning: *Communication, Culture, Connections, Comparisons,* and *Communities,* these bilingual songs integrate skill development through exciting rhythms and melodies that also provide a real-world context for cultural understanding.

Students will improve literacy, vocabulary, reading, and comprehension skills through the rules and examples in this lyrics book. This program works well for learners with diverse learning styles, backgrounds, and disciplines. The lessons can be carried into many areas of study, and more importantly, go beyond the classroom and become part of students' lives at home and in the community.

Enjoy it! *Amusez-vous!*

This learning kit has three components: an audio CD, a 48 page lyrics book and an optional 64 page resource book. They can be used separately, however, if used in tandem, better results will be obtained.

All of the songs in this volume can be used to teach either French or English. The bonus instrumental tracks, which are included on the CD, further boost language fluency as students use the lyrics book to perform "karaoke" style.

A few ways to use this resource:

This resource works well as both a remedial tutorial and as an enriching curriculum supplement.

In the classroom:

- ☑ Have beginning students listen while using the lyrics book. Later, have them sing along.

- ☑ Encourage confident students to perform "karaoke style" with the music accompaniment tracks.

- ☑ Advanced students may use the music tracks to create and perform original lyrics (boosting their writing skills).

- ☑ Employ the "cloze" method of learning by "whiting out" some of the words (using a photocopied sheet of lyrics) and have students fill in the words while listening.

At home or in the car:

- ☑ Whether you listen on the family stereo, through a stereo headset, or in the car, *Bilingual Songs: English-French, vol. 4* can be great fun and entertainment for the entire family.

Introduction
L'introduction

chorus/*refrain* :

Hey there brothers. Come and join along!
Hey there sisters. Celebrate in song.

> *Hé! Les copains! Joignez-vous! Venez!*
> *Hé! Les copines! Pour célébrer.*

Learning can be lots of fun
when each thing we learn is sung.
Soon we will learn much more
with *'Bilingual Songs, vol. 4'*.

> *Apprendre peut être amusant*
> *si tout se fait en chantant.*
> *Bientôt nous apprendrons encore*
> *avec «Bilingual Songs, vol. 4».*

chorus/*refrain*...

'You'
«Tu» et «vous»

chorus/*refrain :*

'You', 'you', 'you'
In English it's a simple 'you'.
'You', 'you', 'you'
How are you today?

> «You», «you», «you»
> *En anglais, c'est simplement* «you».
> «You», «you», «you»
> *Comment allez-vous?*

In French there are two ways
that one can say 'you'.
Each situation dictates
the proper form we choose.

We use *«tu»* for a friend.
«Vous» shows respect.
We use *«vous»* for a group.
We're not finished yet.

In the province of Québec
«*tu*» is often used
in formal situations
where others might use «vous».

chorus/*refrain*...

En français il y a
deux façons de dire «you».
Chaque situation te dit
ce que tu choisis.

On dit «*tu*» *pour un ami.*
«*Vous*» *montre le respect*
et «*vous*» *montre le pluriel*
et puis vous choisissez.

Dans la province de Québec,
«*tu*» *au lieu de* «*vous*»
est souvent utilisé
dans la langue parlée.

chorus/*refrain...*

"I'm 'Mr. Leblanc'.
You are my new students."
«*Je m'appelle M. Leblanc.
Vous êtes mes nouveaux élèves.*»

"We'll have lots of fun
but tell me first where you're from."
«*Nous allons nous amuser
mais dites-moi d'où vous venez.*»

"I am Monique from Martinique.
I am pleased to meet you."
«*Je m'appelle Monique de Martinique.
Je suis contente de vous voir.*»

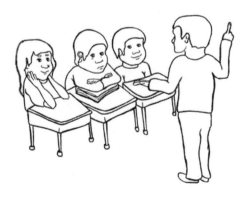

"I am from France. My name is Raúl
and who are all of you?"
>   «*Je viens de France. Je m'appelle Raoul
>   et qui êtes-vous tous?*»

"I am from Egypt. I am Shatir
and where are you from, teacher?"
>   «*Je viens d'Égypte. Je m'appelle Shatir.
>   D'où venez-vous, Monsieur?*»

"I am Mr. Leblanc. I'm from Monaco.
Class is over. Let's go."
>   «*Je m'appelle M. Leblanc de Monaco.
>   La classe est finie. Partons.*»

chorus/*refrain*...

Unisex Nouns
Les noms unisexes

chorus/*refrain* :

'Round and 'round and 'round we go.
Some things change and some things don't.
In French you must remember the gender.
You need to learn these things by rote.

> *Tournons, tournons, tous en rond.*
> *Des choses changent et d'autres pas.*
> *N'oubliez pas le genre en français.*
> *L'apprendre par cœur vous devez.*

Rap:

These professions stay the same
but the preceding articles change.
Ces professions ne changent pas
mais l'article précédent change.

I'm a good cyclist.
Je suis un bon cycliste. (m)
I'm a good cyclist.
Je suis une bonne cycliste. (f)

I'm a good student.
Je suis un bon élève. (m)
I'm a good student.
Je suis une bonne élève. (f)

I'm a good journalist.
Je suis un bon journaliste. (m)
I'm a good journalist.
Je suis une bonne journaliste. (f)

I'm a good tourist.
Je suis un bon touriste. (m)
I'm a good tourist.
Je suis une bonne touriste. (f)

chorus/*refrain* :

I'm the best artist.
Je suis le meilleur artiste. (m)
I'm the best artist.
Je suis la meilleure artiste. (f)

I'm the best astronaut.
Je suis le meilleur astronaute. (m)
I'm the best astronaut.
Je suis la meilleure astronaute. (f)

I'm the best athlete.
Je suis le meilleur athlète. (m)
I'm the best athlete.
Je suis la meilleure athlète. (f)

I'm the best guide.
Je suis le meilleur guide. (m)
I'm the best guide.
Je suis la meilleure guide. (f)

chorus/*refrain* :

Nº 4

To Be
Être

chorus/*refrain* :

Some things about a language
are difficult, you'll see.
In English it's 'contractions';
in French the verb 'to be'.

You can learn them quickly
When you sing along.
«To be» and 'contractions'
seem simple with this song.

Certaines choses dans une langue
semblent difficiles peut-être.
En anglais : les «contractions» ;
en français : le verbe «être».

On peut les apprendre rapidement
et tout en chantant.
«Être» et «les contractions»
s'apprennent facilement.

Rapped:

Je suis à l'école.
I am at school.
I'm at school.

> *Tu n'es pas à l'école.*
> You are not at school.
> You aren't at school.

Il est à l'hôpital.
He is at the hospital.
He's at the hospital.

> *Elle n'est pas à l'hôpital.*
> She is not at the hospital.
> She isn't at the hospital.

Nous sommes au café.
We are at the coffee shop.
We're at the coffee shop.

> *Ils ne sont pas au café.*
> They are not at the coffee shop.
> They aren't at the coffee shop.

Nous sommes à l'hôtel.
We are at the hotel.
We're at the hotel.

> *Elles ne sont pas à l'hôtel.*
> They are not at the hotel.
> They aren't at the hotel.

chorus/*refrain* :

Vous êtes au théâtre.
You are at the theatre.
You're at the theatre.

> *Vous n'êtes pas au théâtre.*
> You are not at the theatre.
> You aren't at the theatre.

Vous êtes à la plage.
You are at the beach.
You're at the beach.

Vous n'êtes pas à la plage.
You are not at the beach.
You aren't at the beach.

L'auto est dans le garage.
The car is in the garage.
It's in the garage.

Le vélo n'est pas dans le garage.
The bike is not in the garage.
It isn't in the garage.

chorus/*refrain* :

Ring, Ring
Dring, dring

chorus/*refrain :*

Thanks for calling.
I'm not home.
Leave your number
after the tone.

It's nice to hear
from all my friends.
I'll call you back
before the day ends.

*Merci de m'avoir
téléphoné.
Laisse ton numéro
après la tonalité.*

*Ça me fait plaisir
d'entendre mes amis.
Je vous rappellerai
en fin de soirée.*

Hi! It's Greg.
Paris is a dream!
01 26 32 12 18
(zero one, twenty-six,
thirty-two, twelve, eighteen)

Salut! C'est Greg. Je suis à Paris.
01 26 32 12 18
(zéro un, vingt-six, trente-deux,
douze, dix-huit)

Call me. It's Suzy.
Hurry, please!
02 15 29 40 33
(zero two, fifteen, twenty-nine,
forty, thirty-three)

C'est Suzy. Appelle-moi.
Dépêche-toi!
02 15 29 40 33
(zéro deux, quinze, vingt-neuf,
quarante, trente-trois)

Did you know?

Telephone numbers in Europe are grouped into
five pairs.

chorus/*refrain* :

Thanks for calling.
I'm not home.
Leave your number
after the tone.

It's nice to hear
from all my friends.
I'll call you back
before the day ends.

*Merci de m'avoir
téléphoné.
Laisse ton numéro
après la tonalité.*

*Ça me fait plaisir
d'entendre mes amis.
Je vous rappellerai
en fin de soirée.*

Hi! It's Ted.
André is with me.
04 11 50 13 23
(zero four, eleven, fifty, thirteen, twenty-three)

*Salut! C'est Ted.
André est avec moi.
04 11 50 13 23
(zéro, quatre, onze, cinquante, treize,
vingt-trois)*

Hi! It's Rose.
Noon sounds great.
03 60 20 13 38
(zero, three, sixty, twenty, thirteen, thirty-eight)

Salut! C'est Rose.
Je suis libre à midi.
03 60 20 13 38
(zéro, trois, soixante, vingt, treize,
trente-huit)

chorus/*refrain* :

Thanks for calling.
I'm not home.
Leave your number
after the tone.

It's nice to hear
from all my friends.
I'll call you back
before the day ends.

Merci de m'avoir
téléphoné.
Laisse ton numéro
après la tonalité.

Ça me fait plaisir
d'entendre mes amis.
Je vous rappellerai
en fin de soirée.

How Often?
Combien de fois?

chorus/*refrain...*

How often do you vacuum?
do you do it frequently?
How often do you read
or go to see a good movie?

> *Combien de fois fais-tu le ménage?*
> *Le fais-tu fréquemment?*
> *Combien de fois lis-tu un livre*
> *ou vas-tu au cinéma?*

"Adverbs of frequency";
describe how often things occur.
"Adverbs of frequency";
they're easy words to learn.

> *«Les adverbes de fréquence» ;*
> *indiquent la fréquence d'une action.*
> *«Les adverbes de fréquence» ;*
> *lequel, c'est la question.*

Rap:

Always	*toujours*
Usually	*d'habitude*
Often	*souvent*
Sometimes	*parfois*
Seldom	*pas souvent*
Rarely	*rarement*
Never	*jamais*

I always work this hard.
I usually run this far.

I often eat too fast.
I sometimes skip a class.

I seldom skate on ice.
I rarely criticize.

I never agonize.
How 'bout you?

Je travaille toujours comme ça.
Je cours d'habitude là.

Je mange souvent rapidement.
Parfois je ne suis pas présent.

Je ne patine pas souvent.
Je critique rarement.

Je ne m'en fais jamais.
Et quant à vous?

chorus/*refrain* :

How often do you vacuum?
Do you do it frequently?
How often do you read
or go to see a good movie?

Combien de fois fais-tu le ménage?
Le fais-tu fréquemment?
Combien de fois lis-tu un livre
ou vas-tu au cinéma?

"Adverbs of frequency";
describe how often things occur.
"Adverbs of frequency";
they're easy words to learn.

«Les adverbes de fréquence» ;
indiquent la fréquence d'une action.
«Les adverbes de fréquence» ;
lequel, c'est la question.

What is Recycling?
Qu'est-ce que le recyclage?

chorus/*refrain* :

Do you know these 'question words'?
WH 'question words'?
Do you know these 'question words'?
They're a snap to use.

> *Connaissez-vous tous ces mots?*
> *Les pronoms interrogatifs?*
> *Connaissez-vous touts ces mots?*
> *Ils sont très faciles.*

Who, what, when, where, why, which.
We'll use these words as we sing
a song about recycling.

> *Qui, que, quand, où, pourquoi, quel.*
> *Ces mots seront utilisés*
> *pour le recyclage. Chantez!*

chorus / *refrain* :

WHO should recycle?
We all should recycle:
you, me and everyone.
A healthy planet is more fun.

> *QUI doit recycler?*
> *On doit tous recycler :*
> *toi, moi, le monde entier,*
> *pour une planète en santé!*

WHAT is recycling?
It's when we reuse things;
saving things that won't decay
and using them in another way.

> *QUE veut dire recycler?*
> *C'est réutiliser*
> *tout ce que nous pouvons et*
> *l'utiliser d'une autre façon.*

chorus/*refrain*...

WHEN should we recycle?
24/7.
If we recycle all the time,
Planet Earth will manage fine.

> *QUAND doit-on recycler?*
> *À tout moment.*
> *Si on recycle tout le temps*
> *la Terre existera longtemps.*

WHERE should we recycle?
Every place we stay.
At home and at school,
recycling is the only way.

> *OÙ doit-on recycler?*
> *Partout où nous allons.*
> *À l'école, à la maison,*
> *recycler est la seule façon.*

WHY should we recycle?
It affects us all.
Recycling is one solution
for the problem of pollution.

> *POURQUOI doit-on recycler?*
> *Cela nous touche tous.*
> *C'est une solution*
> *au problème de la pollution.*

WHICH things can we recycle?
Paper, metal, glass.
Plastic, too. Reduce trash.
If you're confused, be sure to ask.

> *QUELS objets peut-on recycler?*
> *Papier, métal, verre,*
> *plastique aussi. Moins de saleté.*
> *Demandez si vous hésitez!*

chorus / *refrain*...

---

*Quel est un adjectif interrogatif.
Les autres formes sont : quels, quelle, quelles.

How Much? How Many? Combien?

chorus/*refrain :*

A little of this. A little of that.
Being the chef is a treat.
A little of this. A little of that.
I'll make so much to eat.

> *Un peu de ci. Un peu de ça.*
> *Être chef est un plaisir.*
> *Un peu de ci. Un peu de ça.*
> *À manger je vais servir.*

"How much?" "How many?"
In French we only say «*combien*».
"How much?" "How many?"
«*Combien*»'s the word to use.

> *C'est toujours «combien»;*
> *l'adverbe de quantité.*
> *C'est toujours «combien»;*
> *le mot utilisé.*

How much cheese will I use?
How many eggs to choose?
How much sugar do I need?
So many guests to feed.

Combien de fromages utilisés?
Combien d'œufs à acheter?
Combien de sucre me faut-il?
Tant d'invités à nourrir.

chorus/*refrain* :

How much milk will I use?
How many nuts to choose?
How much flour do I need?
So many guests to feed.

Combien de lait utilisé?
Combien de noix à choisir?
Combien de farine faut-il?
Tant d'invités à servir.

chorus/*refrain* :

Pen Pals
Les correspondants

Chorus/refrain : (Male singer)

Hello, pen pal.
What do you say?
I'm pleased to write
to you today.

Let me tell you
a bit about me,
my appearance
and personality.

Salut, mon amie.
Que dis-tu?
Content de t'écrire
aujourd'hui.

Je vais te parler
un peu de moi
de mon aspect
de ma personnalité.

I'm hardworking.
I'm not lazy.
Sometimes my sister
drives me crazy.

She thinks she's shy
but she's not.
She's outgoing
and she talks a lot.

Je travaille dur.
Je ne suis pas paresseux.
Parfois ma sœur
me rend furieux.

Elle se croit timide.
Elle ne l'est pas.
Elle est ouverte et elle
parle tout le temps.

I have curly
dark brown hair.
My eyes are blue.
My skin is fair.

I'm not short.
I am tall.
I love to have fun
playing football.

Mes cheveux bouclés
sont brun foncé.
Mes yeux sont bleus.
Ma peau est claire.

Je ne suis pas petit.
Je suis grand.
J'aime bien jouer
au football.

chorus/*refrain* :

Hello pen pal...

Salut, mon ami. Que dis-tu?
Contente de t'écrire aujourd'hui.

I am short.
I'm not tall.
I don't like
football at all.

My hair is blonde.
My skin is dark.
I like playing frisbee
in the park.

Je suis petite.
Je ne suis pas grande.
Je n'aime pas du
tout le football.

Je suis blonde.
Ma peau est foncée
et au frisbee
j'aime jouer.

I am cheerful.
I'm not boring.
My obnoxious brother's
another story.

He thinks he's weak
but he's strong.
He's at the gym
all day long.

Je suis joyeuse,
pas ennuyeuse.
Mon odieux frère,
c'est une autre affaire.

Il se croit faible,
mais il est musclé.
Il est au gymnase
toute la journée.

Hello, pen pal.
What do you say?
I'm pleased to write
to you today.

Salut, mon ami.
Que dis-tu?
Contente de t'écrire
aujourd'hui.

My Car...
Mon auto ...

My car is big.
It's bigger than your car.
My car is fast.
It's faster than your car... by far.

> Mon auto est grande,
> plus grande que ton auto.
> Mon auto est rapide,
> plus rapide que ton auto... de loin!

My car is sleek.
It's sleeker than your car.
My car's expensive,
more expensive than your car... by far.

> Mon auto est chic,
> plus chic que ton auto.
> Mon auto est coûteuse,
> plus coûteuse que ton auto... de loin!

chorus/*refrain* :

Bigger, faster,
newer, sleeker;
people say:
my car's 'a keeper'.

More expensive,
more efficient,
my car's hot
and your car isn't... by far.

Plus neuve, plus grande
et plus chic.
On dit qu'elle est
plus rapide!
Plus coûteuse,
plus économique!
Mon auto est plus
fantastique...de loin!

My car is new.
It's newer than your car.
My car's more efficient,
more efficient than your car... by far.

Mon auto est neuve,
plus neuve que ton auto.
Mon auto est économique,
plus économique que ton auto... de loin!

My car is clean.
It's cleaner than your car.
My car is fancy.
It's fancier than your car... by far.

Mon auto est propre,
plus propre que ton auto.
Mon auto est fantastique,
plus fantastique que ton auto... de loin!

chorus/*refrain...*

Hey! Wait a minute.
Hold on guy!
My ego's not hurtin'.
I'll tell you why.

You're not for real.
You're all talk.
Your silly car came
from a cereal box!... A toy car!

Hé! Attends une minute.
Écoute mon gars!
Mon égo est intact,
tu sais pourquoi?

Tu es blagueur.
Tu es parleur.
Ta super auto sort
d'une boîte de céréales... Une petite auto!

chorus/*refrain...*

Superlatives
Le superlatif

Chorus/*refrain* :

Superlative adjectives;
we use them when we compare things.
Superlative adjectives;
when we've three things or more.

> *On utilise le superlatif*
> *pour comparer des choses.*
> *On utilise le superlatif*
> *pour plus de deux choses.*

Rap style:

Fastest, tallest,
biggest, smallest,
weakest, finest.
So many we can learn.

> *Le plus rapide, le plus haut,*
> *le plus grand, le plus petit,*
> *le plus faible, le plus chic*
> *sont des superlatifs.*

chorus/*refrain*...

He is strong.
She is stronger,
but their cousin
is the strongest.

Your hair's long.
His is longer.
That kid, there,
has the longest.

Il est fort.
Elle est plus forte
mais leur cousin
est le plus fort.

Tes cheveux sont longs.
Les siens sont plus longs.
Ceux de ce gamin
sont les plus longs.

chorus/*refrain*...

His dog's small.
Hers is smaller
but my puppy
is the smallest.

His mom's tall.
My mom's taller
but their mom
is the tallest.

Son chien est petit.
Le sien est plus petit
mais mon chiot
est le plus petit.

Sa mère est grande.
Ma mère est plus grande
mais leur mère
est la plus grande.

chorus/*refrain*...

My Two Cents
Mes deux sous

Chorus/*refrain* :

Whether it's a statement,
exclamation or a question,
the important thing when speaking is
... the inflection.

> *Si c'est une déclaration,*
> *exclamation ou affirmation,*
> *l'important en parlant c'est*
> *... l'intonation.*

Just the other day
I bought some lunch
and when I stopped to pay:
"How much money
do you have?"
"Two cents."
"Two cents?"
"Yes... Two cents!"

L'autre jour j'ai
acheté à manger
et quand j'ai voulu payer :

«Combien d'argent as-tu?»
        «Deux sous.»
«Deux sous?»
        «Oui... Deux sous!»

chorus/*refrain*...

Just the other day
I bought some books
and when I stopped to pay:
        "How much money
        do you have?"
                "Two cents."
        "Two cents?"
                "Yes... Two cents!"

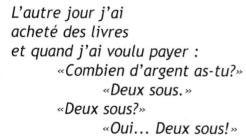

L'autre jour j'ai
acheté des livres
et quand j'ai voulu payer :
        «Combien d'argent as-tu?»
                «Deux sous.»
        «Deux sous?»
                «Oui... Deux sous!»

chorus/*refrain*...

Ask your retailer about other excellent audio programs by teacher, Sara Jordan

Bilingual Songs™ Volumes 1-4

*** Parents' Choice Award Winner! ***

The perfect way to have fun while acquiring a second language. This series teaches the basic alphabet, counting to 100, days of the week, months of the year, colors, food, animals, parts of the body, clothing, family members, emotions, places in the community and the countryside, measurement, opposites, greetings, gender, articles, plural forms of nouns, adjectives, pronouns, adverbs of frequency, question words and much more! ENGLISH-FRENCH and ENGLISH-SPANISH

Songs and Activities for Early Learners™

Dynamic songs teach the alphabet, counting, parts of the body, members of the family, colors, shapes, fruit and more. Helps students of all ages to learn basic vocabulary easily. The kit includes a lyrics book with activities which teachers may reproduce for their classes. IN ENGLISH, FRENCH OR SPANISH

Thematic Songs for Learning Language™

Delightful collection of songs and activities teaching salutations, rooms of the house, pets, meals, food and silverware, transportation, communication, parts of the body, clothing, weather and prepositions. Great for ESL classes. The kit includes a lyrics book with activities teachers may reproduce for their classes. IN ENGLISH, FRENCH OR SPANISH

Reading Readiness Songs™

Comes with a lyrics book which includes helpful hints for parents and teachers. This great introduction to reading uses both phonics and whole language approaches. Topics covered include the alphabet, vowels, consonants, telling time, days of the week, seasons, the environment and more! VERSIONS IN ENGLISH, FRENCH OR SPANISH

Grammar Grooves vol.1™

Ten songs that teach about nouns, pronouns, adjectives, verbs, tenses, adverbs and punctuation. Activities and puzzles, which may be reproduced, are included in the lyrics book to help reinforce learning even further. A complement of music tracks to the 10 songs is included for karaoke performances. Also great for music night productions. IN ENGLISH, FRENCH OR SPANISH

Funky Phonics®: Learn to Read Volumes 1-4

Blending the best in educational research and practice, Sara Jordan's four part series provides students with the strategies needed to decode words through rhyming, blending and segmenting. Teachers and parents love the lessons and activities while children will find the catchy, toe-tapping tunes fun.
IN ENGLISH

Lullabies Around the World

*** Parents' Choice Award Winner! ***

Traditional lullabies sung by native singers with translated verses in English. Multicultural activities are included in the lyrics book. Includes a complement of music tracks for class performances.
Pre-K - Grade 3   11 DIFFERENT LANGUAGES

Healthy Habits™

*** Directors' Choice Award Winner! ***

Songs and activities for Pre-K to Grade 3 covering nutrition, the food pyramid, anatomy, dental hygiene, personal and fire safety. The lyrics book which accompanies the recording has activities which can be reproduced for a class. A complement of music-only tracks works well for performances.
IN ENGLISH

The Presidents' Rap®

from Washington to George W. Bush. The legends of the American Presidents live on in classical, swing, dixie, pop and rap music. A musical treasure trove of tid-bits of information on each President. Very popular among teachers wanting to put on musical shows in their school. IN ENGLISH

The Math Unplugged™ Series

Available for Addition, Subtraction, Division and Multiplication. Tuneful songs teach kids the basic math facts. Repetitive, musical and fun. A great resource. Each audio kit includes a lyrics book with worksheet pages which may be reproduced.
IN ENGLISH

1020405